Northlight

DOUGLAS DUNN

Northlight

faber and faber

LONDON · BOSTON

First published in 1988
by Faber and Faber Limited
3 Queen Square London WC1N 3AU

Photoset by Wilmaset Birkenhead Wirral
Printed in Great Britain by
Richard Clay Ltd Bungay Suffolk

British Library Cataloguing in Publication Data

Dunn, Douglas, *1942–*
Northlight.
I. Title
821'.914
ISBN 0–571–15228–7
ISBN 0–571–15229–5 Pbk

To Baba and Robbie

Contents

Acknowledgements

Acknowledgements are made gratefully to the editors of the following magazines in which some of these poems first appeared: *Antaeus, Cencrastus, Glasgow Herald, London Magazine, Kenyon Review, Numbers, Outcrop, The Poetry Book Society Anthology 1987–8* (Hutchinson), *Poetry Review, Proof, Radical Scotland, TLS, 2 Plus 2*, and *Verse*.

'S. Frediano's' first appeared in *The New Yorker*; 'Going to Aberlemno' appeared on a poster published by Book Trust Scotland; 'December's Door' in a lecture published by the Friends of Edinburgh University Library; '4/4' in the *Proceedings* of the 73rd Conference of the Scottish Library Association, 1987; and 'Memory and Imagination' appeared in the catalogue of an exhibition of the same title organized by the Scottish Arts Council and in *Art International*.

At Falkland Palace

For L.J.B.

Innermost dialect
Describes Fife's lyric hills,
Life, love and intellect
In lucid syllables,
    Domestic air.
Natural play of sun and wind
Collaborates with leaf and mind,
    The world a sentient
    Botanic instrument,
        Visible prayer.
    Everything's birth begins
    On the moment of the May's
    Creaturely origins
    – I'll live for these good days
        Love leads me to
In gardened places such as this
Of the flower and apple-promise,
    Lark-sung, finch-wonderful;
    Edenic circumstance, not fall,
        Walking with you.
    Balladic moments pass,
    Tongue-tied, parochial,
    A narrative of grass
    And stone's hierarchical
        Scottish Versailles.
These native liberties propose
Our lives, rose by unbudding rose,
    A song-crazed laverock
    Whose melodies unlock
        Audible sky.

[1]

Dynastic stonework flakes,
Weathers and fails, withdraws
From shapely time and shakes
A gargoyle's severed claws
    At visitors.
Here wrinkled time's abolished house
Perpetuates a posthumous
    Nation, monarchy's urn
    In which the Stewarts mourn
        What once was theirs.
    In a country like this
    Our ghosts outnumber us:
    A ruined artifice
    Empty and sonorous,
        Malevolent
In how its past force-feeds with filth
Anachronism's commonwealth
    And history bemoans
    What history postpones,
        The true event.
    In the hollows of home
    I find life, love and ground
    And intimate welcome:
    With you, and these, I'm bound
        To history.
Touching your hair, holding your hand,
Your beauty blends with time and land,
    And you are loveliness
    In your green, country dress,
        So fair this day.

Love-making by Candlelight

Skin looked like this two hundred years ago
When candlelight lapped the erotic straw
In hilly farms where windowed candlefire
Burnished imperfect glass. Portending haws
Hung on the leafless bush, amazement's bud
Red on the acres of nocturnal snow
As uplands rose to tufted winterlight,
In their celestial altitude
The eighteenth-century stars.

This is how it must be, shape-shifting fire's
Impatient nudity and ours
On the big bed. A molten vividness
Dismantles gender and the way it moves
Identifies a married venery
Timeless in the bedroom of the species –
A Pictish smile, a medieval kiss,
A whispered pre-industrial draught
On our contemporary bed.

Played on by fire, those clustered cornice grapes
Outwit their plaster: cornucopia's vine,
Pompeian opulence, rumours
From far back, echoes of Florentine
Intrigue, Renaissance footsteps in the hall
Where gossips overhear indelible
Echoed courtships; and these Muscovian furs
Were linen until fire reshaped
Their transient destiny.

[3]

Hands dipped in light-and-shadow cast
Ledas and satyrs on the bedroom wall.
A candleflame's a silent chatterbox
And cinematic book: bestiary candle,
History candle, yellow metaphor,
Venereal fire. Open the curtains now
And add a star to what we do and say
Past midnight in our only country,
Our private anywhere.

Who else is looking at the Firth tonight
Drowsy with afterlove? Local Tristan,
Indigenous Iseult, and Dido sees
Aeneas in a navigation light.
Dog-collared Abelard walks Heloise
Among the gravestones, yews and cypresses.
An Orphic nightbird cries 'Eurydice'. . .
Love, touch my heart with who you are
And sleep, history, sleep.

S. Frediano's

S. Frediano is St Finnian
Who spelled the rivers with his wand of faith,
The Ayrshire Garnoch and the streams of Down.

He brought his water-miracles to Tuscany,
Turning the Serchio with a little rake,
Praying, perhaps, when it was done, in Gaelic.

Lucca was lonely but not foreign
Far from his college on the coast of Solway,
Candida Casa's Gallovidian stone.

He lies under the high altar
In a faint aroma of cypress,
His bones united by fine silver wires.

It is cool and dark in S. Frediano's church.
Parishioners pray in its visited sanctity,
Listlessly, pious, old, *simpatico*.

Tourists listen in on telephones
To stories in the language of their choice.
There is that smell of medieval history.

I hear a bird high in a vitreous blur
Singing its song of the sacred windows,
Its coincidental literature.

S. Zita, mummified, is dressed
For blessed waltzing when the trumpets sound.
Her skin is fastened like a frozen dust,

Her fingerjoints a grey bamboo,
Her gown a lace spun by celestial spiders,
Bridal, bizarre, miraculous.

In her glass coffin, she exhibits
Centuries of death that mount and mount.
Light Italian lire clink in the coinboxes.

It is a human place – a tourist
Stooped in a pose of scholarly inspection;
A couple who light candles for their dead

And who have yet to read
S. Frediano learned his miracles
In places they came here to be away from.

The People Before

I've turned my back on Tuesday's half-past four
As 1985's obscured momentum
Falters towards the closing of an epoch.
Crepuscular, two tradesmen, walking home,
Know that they're woodcuts by a local master,
Firm local lines, modernity unstuck.

Migrating geese, in an up-ended V,
Caricature my watch's measurement,
Half-past the hour and continuity
In sepia, any time but this
Post-dated country etched in aquatint
Nearing the day of luck and all good wishes.

Streetlamps come on.
Frock-coated decades trespass on the tense.
Spent eras stain
Anachronistic stone –
Luminous echoes, gaslit reminiscence,
Distorted, thinned, Victorian.

A push can coax our gate
Into releasing an Edwardian squeak.
December's frozen rose
Nods to unseen applause.
A sparrow lifts its startled featherweight
And petals tumble in a cruel slapstick.

Preliminary moonlight on the Firth
Casts in-betweenness on the time and light –
Not now, not then, not day, not night,
But moonlight's childhood, waterworn;
And, in one moment, all death, all birth,
All dying and being reborn.

Beyond our neighbours' frosted washing-lines,
Their silvered slates and chimneypots,
Our borderland begins
As light withdraws to loss of Monifieth,
Subplots and counterplots
Narrated in the coastline's myth.

Make what you can of it, for no one knows
What story's told by winter-misted hills
Or how a river flows
Against the tide in white scribbles.
A patiently daemonic frost
Sharpens its needles on the eastern coast.

Processionals of lives go by
On delicate, crisp treads;
Blurred fragrances, gently percussive,
Stir among leaves.
Top-hatted heads of firms and kitchen-maids
Visit the instincts of the eye.

Swish, hush and microsound, the whispered *ahs*,
Converse with silence's midpoint
Over the Firth, and time is disobedient,
Mixing its years and generations.
It's 1940 on the weatherglass
And now and then in the events of nations.

Night swells with navigation's stars
Honed to a masterpiece of quiet.
Dismantled commerce hungers for its jute,
Esparto, timber, coal and mariners,
Prosperity and credit.
Lighthouses warn the swimmers on a lost trade route.

A candleflame, held by a child
Walking past, reddens a window, her face
A spectral captive in the window's glass,
Her neck a ruff of fiery nightgown lace.
Coniferous estates, the winterfield,
Submerge their farms in foliage and grass.

More geese rant westward, flock by chevroned flock.
The house of us now, love, of you and me.
I turn a blacksmithed key in its lock.
Feeling its freezing metal on their hands,
These other people turned this iron key.
The lunar honey fell on Buddon Sands.

February

Maternal in the glow of shaded light,
Your smile has proved the truth of love tonight,
Holding the hunger of our much-loved child
Who lately in his father's arms was held.

Daylight

The big white arms of dawn are cool
In their embrace, and merciful
First blue dispels the estuary's
Possessive, tenemented greys.
The gleam on Buddon Ness protects
Survival where sunlight reacts
With sand and private history,
With window-coloured dawn and sea.
Enormous world, this little place
Observes its vulnerable trace
On time, topography and globe,
Its rooftops polished in the scrub
Of climbing sunlight, while the gleam
On Buddon Ness persists, a dream
In sleepy eyes at windows where
Early risers pause and stare
At distances beyond their town,
And someone in a dressing-gown
Eavesdrops as mysteries discuss
Sung mornings to no human purpose.
Wordless symposia, in tongues
Informed beyond mere rights and wrongs;
Luminous discourse, shade by shade,
Its meanings light-and-water-made
Or turned by wind and by what happens
Into a foliated sense –
A mind could catch at them, and try
To understand that dot of sky
Balanced on Buddon's easternmost
Outreach of military coast

Transmitting random ironies
Out of the library of days.
I've seen a star poised on the tip
Of a still leaf, pure partnership
Here makes with there and everywhere
Between life, death and forever.
Last night in Tayport, leaf and star
– Still, very still – melted together
In life's delight and woke to this
Lucidity and genesis,
A worldlight in the watery grey,
Sinister, thrawn, the estuary
A colourless mirroring stone,
Offensive, querulous, sullen;
And then daylight on Buddon Ness,
Curative, clear and meaningless.

Going to Aberlemno

By archaeologies of air,
Folkways of kirks and parishes
Revised by salty haar,
You reach the previous
Country, the picturesque
And the essential east,
By a padlocked summer kiosk
And industry's ill-starred
Inlets, a breaker's-yard
A ruby sore of rust.
Here four roads intersect
Beside the tallest oak
And the best hawthorn
Where every step you take
Breaks on an acorn.
Through astral solitude
A Pictish dialect,
Above a bridged Firth, cries
For lyric nationhood,
And horsemen, in a stone disguise,
Ride through the Pictish wood.

Abernethy

Air-psalters and pages of stone
Inscribed and Caledonian
Under these leaf-libraries where
Melodious lost literature
Remembers itself! A white
Dove climbs on its Columban flight
In the botanic radiance,
Northlight's late druidic rinse
Lapping against time and earth
In this root view of Fife and Perth.
A thousand years of briars enclose
A wild and matrilinear rose
Whose house began before the oak
First felt the axeman's stroke.
An unrecorded Kentigern
Disturbs a prehistoric fern
And hours from the Pictavian clock
Measure the lives of land and rock
And miles before the pedlared road
Winds of Iona and to God.

Out of the thanages, mormaerdoms,
Legendary shires and kingdoms,
Defunct boundaries and the lost
Dynastic certainties – a ghost
Light on the grass, a shivering
Transparent wing.
Listen to twigs scratch as a broom
Swishes across a vanished room
Trembling on this venerable

And enigmatic hill.
At the time when our names began
In the years of the Dark Age swan
And the wolf, on hills like this one,
A herdsman looked over and down
On blue waters in the strath.
This moment is his aftermath
Also, a lived and living scent
Scattering and ever-present,
As are the lady and her hind
Fragments of spirit, leaf and mind.

75°

I

Delayed by southern possessiveness,
The summer's agents turn up late
With their sorries, their more-or-less
Sincere apologies, lightweight
Attire, ubiquitous assistants
Performing aerial events,
Weavers of avian cradles where
A byre or gable tucks the air
Under its eaves. 'What kept you, friends?'
Bavarian asparagus,
Burgundian grapes and other godsends,
The usual Hispanic fuss,
Devonian nativities
Beginning in the apple trees.
The glass farms of the Netherlands
Commanded sun and tied our hands.
'At least, you've come. Our bad selves, dulled
By winter and frustrated spring,
Drained good from us, and poured a cold
Malevolence over everything.'

II

We tend our earthen restaurants,
Buying our portions of the south;
Strange languages visit our tongues,
Saying 'I love you', mouth to mouth.
Erotic gardens promise fruit
Nurtured from an ancestral root.
A smile, and the clematis flowers.
A few weeks more, and south is ours!
Yachts multiply; pods flex
Deserved and succulent harvests.
Lawn-mowers, shirt-sleeves, open necks . . .
Young girls ring daisies round their wrists.
Mrs Belle Gilsand's parrot squawks
For liberty beyond her clock's
North-facing mantelpiece – humdrum,
Tick-tocking tropic martyrdom.
Deep in coniferous woods, the dry
Needle blankets shift, claw and squall
Shaded by wing-beats, then a shy
Creaturely panic and paw-fall.

III

Eat fern seed, walk invisible.
Summer is fragrant this far north.
By night, on Inverdovat's hill,
Visit the gods of wood and Firth
By paths of inner wanderlust
Here on the summer's Pictish Coast
Where half-forgotten festivals
Quicken the half-remembering pulse.
Watch starlight struggle in an oak's
Irradiated rafters, hear
A minstrelsy from lunar hammocks
Sing love songs to the hemisphere.
Moonbathe, be moonstruck, watch a birch
Assume serenity and search
For its perfection, northern
On its grass sofa, turf and moon-fern
Delighted where a foot-snapped twig
Startles symphonic foliage
And mushrooms tremble on their log,
Stellar on an eternal ridge.

IV

The heart stays out all night. Each house
A variant of moonlit slates
And flightpaths of the flittermouse,
Sleeps in the dream it illustrates
Translating garden laureates
Into unlettered alphabets,
Holding antiquity and now
Within the same nocturnal vow –
Internal wonders in that pale
Hour after sunset when you hear
A visionary nightingale
Articulate your life's frontier.
An owl perched on a chimneypot
Too-woos its legendary thought
Across the estuary of dream
Along the light-buoy's punctual beam.
Stars in the trees, moon on a headstone,
Night's footprints on the riddled earth;
The wind's herbaceous undertone,
Moon-puddled water, mystic Firth . . .

V

Planthouses force Italian heat
On melon, pepper, peach and vine
And horticultural conceit
Perfects a Scottish aubergine.
Imagination manufactures
A vitreous continent, nature's
Geography turned inside out
On the botanic roundabout.
By fraudulent, glass-roofed lagoons
Gardeners ply the trowel and hoe
On Polynesian afternoons
Of the oriole and the papingo.
Waterfalls slacken, their cold threads
Dribble on shrunken riverbeds.
There's trouble at the reservoir:
At night it launders one pale star.
Dry pelts diminish on the road,
Each beast its dehydrated shroud;
A butterfly's life-episode
Withers in daylong adulthood.

VI

Postponed by seasonal delight
And midnight sun, the north returns,
A furred, Icelandic anchorite
Travelling south by landmarked cairns,
Islands, headlands, bearing his cold
Autumnal charms, spelling ridged gold
Into the shiver in the leaf,
Deciduous, wrinkled and skew-whiff.
Rumoured by clouds and sudden chills,
By falls of apple, plum and pear,
Arched, orphaned cats on window-sills
And by botanic disrepair –
Look to your blessings and your coat,
Gloves for your hands, a scarf for your throat.
Your gardens, yielding pod by pod,
Surrender to another god.
Go home; chop wood. North-easters strain
Over the sea. Farewell. This line –
Greybreaking, late September rain –
Falls heavy, cold, and argentine.

Tay Bridge

A sky that tastes of rain that's still to fall
And then of rain that falls and tastes of sky . . .
The colour of the country's moist and subtle
In dusk's expected rumour. Amplify
All you can see this evening and the broad
Water enlarges, Dundee slips by an age
Into its land before the lights come on.
Pale, mystic lamps lean on the river-road
Bleaching the city's lunar after-image,
And there's the moon, and there's the setting sun.

The rail bridge melts in a dramatic haze.
Slow visibility – a long train floats
Through a stopped shower's narrow waterways
Above rose-coloured river, dappled motes
In the eye and the narrow piers half-real
Until a cloud somewhere far in the west
Mixes its inks and draws iron and stone
In epic outlines, black and literal.
Now it is simple, weathered, plain, immodest
In waterlight and late hill-hidden sun.

High water adds freshwater-filtered salt
To the aquatic mirrors, a thin spice
That sharpens light on Middle Bank, a lilt
In the reflected moon's analysis.
Mud's sieved and drained from pewter into gold.
Conjectural infinity's outdone
By engineering, light and hydrous fact,
A waterfront that rises fold by fold
Into the stars beyond the last of stone,
A city's elements, local, exact.

Apples

I eat an apple, skin, core and pips,
And sleep at night the way a yokel sleeps
With thyme and borage in my palliasse,
Lavender pillows in the house of grass.

Apples of Portnauld, scarlet, round and good,
Ripened, come autumn, into savoury
Pleasures. I picked, then chewed in solitude
Behind the crumbling wall, out of the way.

I don't know why I should remember this –
Perhaps the pippin was enough to do it
With its hard flesh, delicious, bitten kiss.
I sit tonight and it is very quiet.

Broughty Ferry

Under the eaves, Elysian icicles
Taper towards stilled drips. In my garden
A naked birch looks lacquered by a hand
Expert in Christmas things or fairyland
Translations. Clever frost has hardened lace
On spiderwebs and shrubs. It has blinded glass
All over the planthouse, and spelled a rose
Into a shuttered bud.

On Broughty Ferry's mansioned slopes, houses
Address the sun I set my eye by, stepping
Through wintry trees, and there's an hour to go
Before the roselight comes to fill the sky.
Yesterday's money celebrates its stone
With watery, cold, imperial
Throwbacks to somewhere else, a hesitant
Refrigerated Orient.

I came home through the Country Bus Station
Eager for half-past-one and views from Fife.
A winey down-and-out, his poly bag
No bundle for a shouldered stick, outstared
Distaste and sentiment, a holly sprig
Defiant in his cap of weathered tweed.
A well-dressed mother with her hand-held son
Resented being there and looked away.

A simpleton went through a dance routine
Shuffling on the cold tiles of the alcove,
Pulling the faces of a mind content

With suffering's low comedy.
A one-legged pigeon hopped between the queues
With messages from Orphic pauperdom.
Cherubic sparrows huddled in their rags.
Policewomen struggled with a runaway.

Inspectors helped a blind man on a bus,
Then when their backs were turned, got off again,
Chasing white probes with thirst or memory.
Young men and women swaggered on the platform,
Loitering, discontent and ghetto-blasting.
Old women, frightened by the depot's
Aroma'd roar, fingered their counted change
Or checked their travel passes, passports home.

My comfortable, mind-aggrandized visions
Melt in the light and then my eyes play tricks
Or beauty tricks my eyes into conceit:
I won't disfigure loveliness I see
With an avoidance of its politics.
Although the silvered rust of docken seed
Shows it has none, nor whitened, brittle grass,
That isn't true of Broughty Ferry's stone,

Improved by roselight's neutral flawlessness,
Dismissing what I think of what I see
Into a stunned perfection, remote,
Depopulated and complacent.
I think of incomes and prosperity.
It comes to Wednesday's rhymed phrase
Holding together versions of events,
Significance that beauty can't erase.

Here and There

'Everybody's got to be somewhere.'
Woody Allen

You say it's mad to love this east-coast weather –
I'll praise it, though, and claim its subtle light's
Perfect for places that abut on water
Where swans on tidal aviaries preen their whites.
You whisper in the south that even the rain
Wins my affection, and I won't deny it,
Watching it drench my intimate domain:
I love the rain and winds that magnify it.
The evening's paper-boy goes round the doors
At his hour of November when the day's
Closing in goose-cries and the sycamores
Darken to silhouettes by darker hedges –

I love that too. '*Provincial*', you describe
Devotion's minutes as the seasons shift
On the planet: I suppose your diatribe
Last week was meant to undercut the uplift
Boundaries give me, witnessed from the brae
Recording weather-signs and what birds pass
Across the year. More like a world, I'd say,
Infinite, curious, sky, sea and grass
In natural minutiae that bind
Body to lifetimes that we all inhabit.
So spin your globe: Tayport is Trebizond
As easily as a regenerate

Country in which to reconstruct a self
From local water, timber, light and earth,
Drawing the line (this might please you) at golf

[26]

Or watersports on a sub-Arctic Firth.
It matters where you cast your only shadow,
And that's my answer to, *'Why did you choose*
Grey northland as your smalltown El Dorado?
You've literature and a career to lose . . .'
It isn't *always* grey. And what is grey?
A colour like the others, snubbed by smart
Depressives who can't stroll an estuary
Without its scope of sky bleaching their hearts.

'. . . You'll twist your art on the parochial lie.'
I love the barbed hush in the holly tree.
'An inner émigré, you'll versify,
Not write. You'll turn your back on history.'
Old friend, you're good for me, but what I want's
Not what your southern bigotry suspects.
Here on imagination's waterfronts
It's even simpler: fidelity directs
Love to its place, the eye to what it sees
And who we live with, and the *whys* and *whens*
That follow *ifs* and *buts*, as, on our knees,
We hope for spirit and intelligence.

Turbulence reaches here: the RAF
Loosens the earwax – so, not paradise
Unless you're awkward, Tory, daft or deaf
Or dealing in destruction's merchandise.
I hold my infant son at the window.
Look, there's the blue; I show him sky and the leaf
On the puddle. What does a baby know
Of the hazardous world? An acrid *if*
Diseases happiness, the damned *perhaps*
Perfected by the uniforms of State.
Our sunlit roofs look nothing on their maps

Other than pulverable stone and slate.
A ferry town, a place to cross from . . . Verse
Enjoys connections: fugitive Macduff
Escaped Macbeth by it. Lacking his purse,
He paid in bread – The Ferry of the Loaf . . .
'Ferries? Fairies! That's medieval farce!'
The wizard, Michael Scot, was born near here . . .
'I might have guessed you'd more like that, and worse . . .'
. . . Alchemist, polymath, astrologer
To the Holy Roman Empire; Tayport's son
Mastered all knowledge, too controversial
For Dante who invented his damnation
In the *Inferno*: 'Tayport Man in Hell,'

They'd say in the *Fife Herald* – 'Sorcerer
From Tayport Slandered by Tuscan Poet.'
*'Worse than parochial! Literature
Ought to be everywhere . . .'* Friend, I know that;
It's why I'm here. My accent feels at home
In the grocer's and in Tentsmuir Forest.
Without a Scottish voice, its monostome
Dictionary, I'm a contortionist –
Tongue, teeth and larynx swallowing an R's
Frog-croak and spittle, social agility,
Its range of fraudulence and repertoires
Disguising place and nationality.

*'What's this about Tayport's centenary?
I never thought you'd prime a parish pump.'*
Not me. Who's said I have? *'It's scenery
You're there for.'* No, it isn't. *'Mugwump!'*
You're wrong again, old friend. Your Englishness
Misleads you into Albionic pride,
Westminstered mockery and prejudice –

You're the provincial, an undignified
Anachronism. The Pax Britannica's
Dismissed, a second-rate Byzantium,
Self-plundered inner empire's Age of Brass.
No houseroom's left in the imperial slum.

And as for scenery, what's wrong with love's
Preferred country, the light, water and sky
Around a town, centennial removes
From time? – The universe within the eye,
Cosmogyny, not parish-governed stars
Cultured above the Tay, but seen from here
When late-night amateur philosophers
Puzzle the substance of their hemisphere.
Time, space and yours truly: all men deserve
Somewhere, if only that, fruition's place,
Quotidian but extra, on a curve
That's capable of upwards into grace,

Eccentric elegance, the personal life
Sharing its ordinariness of days
With speculative spirit which is midwife
To nation, intellect and poetry's
Occurrence. *'You're looking for a chance to wear*
A three-piece suit in tweeds with heavy brogues,
Rehearsing presbyterian despair
On a shoreline, in Reithean monologues.'
So what, if I talk to myself in the woods?
'Perverse retreat into the safe and small
Suggests fake self-denial.' These latitudes
Enlarge me, comfort me, and make me whole.

'No, you're evasive, knowing it might be wrong
To hedge ambition into quietude

[29]

That serves a lowered will with local song,
Beachcombing an iambic neighbourhood.'
It serves my loyalty. It serves increase.
I'll keep no secrets from you: it serves love;
It serves responsibility and caprice.
Damn all careers; I'd rather *be* than *have*.
'You mean, it serves you right?' I hope so, friend.
Pay me a visit and we'll drink to life
One evening when the light and water blend
On the conjectural points of coastal Fife.

Come by the backroads with a sense of time.
Come like Edward Thomas on a holiday
In search of passages of wild-flowered rhyme
No Scot or Irishman would dare betray.
Now, though, I'm going out to the black twigs,
Shy waterbuds reflecting as they drop
To the neighbourly, where the good ground swigs
Any libation from its earthen cup.
Scottishness, if you say so; but I see
Plurals and distances in voiceless wet
Enough to harbour all my history
Inside a house protected from regret.

December's Door

in memoriam Philip Larkin

I kept a church leaf, wishing it were blossom.
    Hull's undressed roadside sycamores
Waded through brittle drifts from Cottingham
    To Newland Park, the still striders.
That leaf still marks my place, but it was worn
    Before I put it there; now dust
Dirties the page, and sinews, strong as thorn,
    Impress the paper's softer crust,
Fragments hanging from them, leaves of a leaf
    Preserved into a second autumn.
Afterwards' keepsake, its botanic grief
    Crumbles in death's *ad infinitum*.

A rudimentary, unclouded sky:
    That day in Hull, your funeral,
I watched rubescent figments vitrify
    On library windows, unreal
Emblems of warehoused English literature
    On the Fifth Floor, and saw again –
When I was in my twenties, I worked there –
    Hull's hazily Utopian green
Purpled and pinkened in a luminous
    Record of seasons. Long straight roads
Reached out across nocturnal Holderness,
    The sea and the visitless woods.

A leaf-marked book aches on my windowsill.
    Straw gold and central green were there
A year ago, but book-locked winterkill
    Disfigured them in printed air.

[31]

In a closed shadow, opened now, a door
    Into December's estuary
Beneath a wigged moon, it honeys the floor
    To starry oak, reflected Tay.
Geese draw their audible, Siberian bow
    Over the moon and Buddon Ness,
And now I can't repay the debt I owe,
    A withered leaf, a dry distress.

Sorrow's vernacular, its minimum,
    A leaf brought in on someone's shoe
Gatecrashed the church in muffled Cottingham,
    Being's late gift, its secret value
A matter of downtrodden poetry,
    Diminutive, and brought to this
By luck of lyric and an unknown tree.
    A passer-by was bound to notice
Crisp leaves at work when everyone had gone,
    Some fricative on paving-stones
As others flecked a winter-wrinkled lawn,
    Remote, unswept oblivions.

Winkie

'We also serve'

GIVE ME GOOD PIGEONS!
You pose in your glass case
Putting a brave face on your taxidermed
Municipal afterlife.
Close by you, Winkie, is a photograph,
A bomber's aircrew snapped in the Second War.
You were their mascot and survival kit.
    Click-click went their tongues;
    And *Winkie-Winkie* they sang
Pressing titbits through the wooden bars
On leather and vibrating fingers.
Winkie-Winkie chirped the goggled men.

Over Norway, its fuselage and wings on fire,
The bomber droned down to the sea,
    Flames sizzling in sleet
    As frantic signals pinged
Against deaf radio ears in nowhere.

Cupped hands released you from a rubber boat.
    Miniature of instinct,
    Dedicated one, your stuffed breast swells
    With pride in your only nature!

GIVE ME GOOD PIGEONS!
Their *chuck-chuck-chuck's*
A thwarted cooing from the woods
Haunting city squares
Named for dimwits and dignitaries
With old bucolic neighbourhoods,
Fife, Gowrie and the Mearns.
Whether as spy-birds on a sneaky errand
Bearing a snip of microfilm for eyes
Devoted to secrecy, released by a hand
Clandestinely over a window-sill in Warsaw,
Or with the gentler mail of love, birth and death
Winged over the suburbs and snipers from
The besieged city – see the rifle, the Prussian eye
Point through the foliage round the gardened villas –
    You are liberty's bird,
    Unstreamlined and civilian,
    With the guts and stamina of a taxpayer
And behind you the solidarity of your species,
    The Universal Union of Pigeons.

    Your mission doesn't matter
    Nor what unvisa'd coasts
    You cross on your postal expeditions,
Nor the direction you take, or whatever
Nationality is claimed for the forests below
Or who pretends to own the air and seasons
And the pronunciation of rivers and mountains.
    The blame is not yours –
    Docile legionary,
    Warrior bearing words,
    Beloved of the Intelligence Services'
    Eccentric dogsbodies,
    Dovecote attendants

[34]

In the obscurest ministerial spires
With their bowls and jugs, their bags of maize
For kept cushats, *pigeons voyageurs*, homers,
Birds of the cloak-and-dagger cryptography.

An imprisoned lover turns on his stinking straw
And a dove at the window chortles.
A letter is read to the sound of cooing.

I do not like the big brave boasts of war.
        GIVE ME GOOD PIGEONS! –
A very large number of Great Commoners
Built like Nye Bevan or Gambetta.

        Winkie read his charts
On his table of instinct, and found the Tay's dent
        On the planet of places.
        A perfect rescue – saved by a bird
        Homing down to Carnoustie.

Bird of X-marks-the-spot
Bird of the ringed foot, married to the miles
Bird of human purpose but immune to guilt
Bearer of tidings and long-distance billet-doux
Reports of troop movements, the planned assassination
Scorner of moats, guard towers and jammed radio
Dove that to a hand in Babylon
Brought more news of the strange horsemen
And bird that to Chaucerian casements brought
Melodious greetings to the heartsick Lady
Bird of the allotments, bird of the long race
Hand-held bird, heartbeat in gentle hands
Olympic bird, love-bird, bird of the peace
Dove of the Annunciation, forerunner of Christ

[35]

Bird of the strange beam and the beautiful lily
Mendicant bird, begging around footwear
With your jabbing head, your hungry, urban strut

FLY, WINKIE, FLY!

Muir's Ledgers

Men hurry in a scuff of studs down cobbled wynds,
Heads bent in a dark morning, blowing on their hands.
The Firth-side farms are fleeing from the winter salts;
Defrosting hammers, skin and fire on nuts and bolts
Elaborate their work-noise in the river's yards.
From their Italianated villas, river-lords
Look out on blueing mountains and relaxing yachts;
Self-made propriety's bucked up in morning suits.
Left angry wives, with bairns, in smells of breakfast,
Are unaware the winter light is colourist,
Although kimono'd wives, whose children are at school
In England, buy pictures from Peploe, Hunter and Cadell.
Now Edwin Muir walks from the tram to be a clerk
In Renfrew where the river flows like liquid work
Past Lobnitz's, a shipyard where his writing fills
Commercial ledgers with lists of materials.
Doves on a ledge, a corner of town hall baronial,
Remind him of the future life he'll live in verses
Which, one day, he'll write, in towns other than this.

A House in the Country

'O God! I could be bounded in a nut-shell, and count myself
a king of infinite space, were it not that I have bad dreams.'
Hamlet

Not Scotland. The colour of the stone
Remembers somewhere *sur Vézère*
Or Tuscany, the Serchio's watertone
Italianate among the cocklebur.

Unopened years burst loose, an iron gate
Inched on its hindered arc, its squeak
Increasing as my bodyweight
Crushes its rust through cry to scream and shriek.

A sore path, and illegible:
Its arrow-headed thorns nip legs and hands –
Red-beaded bracelets and a scratched standstill
Waist-deep in brambled reprimands.

The door's decayed and locked: flaked paint and rust,
Negative timbers on which wood-weeds cling,
One in flower. A doorpost
Crumbles on toe-touch, shuddering.

A kick would smash this door.
I look around and wonder where I am,
Hearing my blood percuss, the red drummer,
Then find a key cold on my sweating palm.

Webs lace the narrow hall. Floorboards protest
At the weight of my shadow, disgruntled
Cries that release an insect ghost,
Digested flies on a transparent scaffold.

[38]

A joist gives on my afterstep. Wood quits
Its fastenings. House-sounds reverberate
In a grey resonance as powdery minutes
Clamour for quiet and then hesitate

On their hazards, blinking in light
Shuttered until now, sneaking
Through keyholes, under doors, off-white
On plaster puddles, the whole house creaking.

A sitting room's dust-sheeted furniture
Dwells on its family thoughts in indoor silence,
The frequency on which its spiders hear
Their lives and predatory conversations

Passing down lifetimes, polyphonic with
Remembered chit-chat or a chair's
Collected memories. Piano breath
Withdraws into its contemplated quavers.

Books and a desk; a jacket's shape
Transforms a chair into a studious shrug,
An amputated, headless stoop
Mouthing a dusty monologue,

Pulling the darkness down
As seasons, politics and swallows pass
And natural and human transformation
Recur on dusty window-glass.

In swirls of air and daylight alien
To it, reluctantly, the room confronts
Sky, wind and summer's herbal rain,
Noise, light and celebrants.

A grey globe ponders on its plinth,
A sphere within a varnished O's embrace
Hugging the planetary labyrinth,
Its cuddled continents all out of place.

Webs fold and curdle in the sunlit wind's
Expulsion of the shadows, and a man
Appears from nowhere or the mind's
Liberty to be more than one.

I am nowhere, everywhere and past
In a house in a country I do not know
A stone clock on the mantel grinds to dust
Minutes that were lifetimes long ago

'No, not that door,'
He says. 'Look at your mirrored face.
You'll learn you've visited that room before
In other houses in another place.

'Reality's the ghost
Stalking your privacy and footsteps
With minstrelsies. Your innermost
Identity eavesdrops

'On what it does and where it goes with you
Among the flowers and clocks, perfidy, faith,
The groves of rooms that utter you
Beyond the physical and into death.'

And then he says again: 'No, not that door.'
Skeletal alphabets
Drop from their bookshelves to the rubbled floor,
Trash *videlicets*

Dismembered from their etymologies,
Words and the shards of an unspoken word,
Lost mouths and dumb debris
Emaciated and disordered.

Hereafter's solitary, rooted to
His captive afterlife disturbed by me,
He spins his globe, and dust-clouds clear to blue
Oceans, greens continents and history.

Imagined stranger, I am in your house
By ways of sleep and owls, and you know why
The door you guard's the door I have to choose
Before my cowardice becomes a lie.

A Snow-walk

What's haunting what, the birchwood or the snow?
It feels too European – this high, barbed fence,
A dog barking, a shot, and the sub-zero
Mid-winter rippled by a mortal cadence.

The water-tower near McGregor's house
Rejects its hurtful simile and slips
Behind the blizzard's curtain – ominous,
Re-memoried or rumoured guardianships.

White shelves on cypresses; and history's
Gaunt silver on a feathered crucifix –
A hawk nailed by its wings, a predatory
Snow-narrative retold in dead athletics.

Large tree-stumps, scattered through a chain-sawed wood,
Metamorphose to dust-cloth'd furniture,
Closed forest rooms, palatial solitude,
Iced armchairs and a branch-hung chandelier.

That fence again; a sign – *Guard Dogs Patrolling*.
Embedded in the snow, low huts appear,
A disused railway line, the shed for coaling,
A toppled goods van and a snow-filled brazier.

Home feels a life away and not an hour
Along the length of an industrial fence,
By friendly holdings and a water-tower
Robbed of simplicity and innocence.

Jig of the Week No. 21

Under optimum conditions – the room quiet
In fireglow, rain lashing on nocturnal glass –
I start an old American puzzle.
It smells like my Webster's dictionary;
It reminds me of the lesson in Latin
Translating Lincoln's *Gettysburg Address*
Into my Ciceronian of errors.
On junior versions of wet, wintry nights
Around Christmas, I tried to be patient,
A jigsaw on a white enamel tray
Encouraging pictorial wanderlust –
My father's ear close to the wireless set's
Hummed murmuring of Cold War '49,
My mother sewing, my brother fast asleep.
Posed by the artist in a daze of stunned
Courage, a wounded man waves in the paint,
A salutation from a grassy foreground.
Here is a piece of sky; this one's a hoof.
I give a man his legs, then rummage for
A clue of horse, a clump of grass. Slaughter's
Perfectionists, the North Virginian troops
March through the woods of Pennsylvania
Intent on orders and aesthetic war.
Omniscient history makes good puzzles:
This one is *Pickett's Charge at Gettysburg*.
Jigsaw research – whose side was Pickett on?
I look him up, then file a book away.
The man who painted this supported Blue;
My mind and fingers soldier with the Grey.
Three hundred fragments of American

Cardboard carnage! This old Bostonian box
Crossed the Atlantic sixty years ago;
Thousands went all over the United States
Shipped by the Universal Distribution Company.
A segment finishes the Stars and Stripes
Carried before blue-trousered infantry.
A dozen pieces, more or less the same,
Assemble shell bursts, foliage and sky,
Turquoise and pink, a summer's afternoon
On Cemetery Ridge, the Butcher's Bill
Extortionate in fact but not in paint –
Invoices brought at night, slipped under doors.
A painter oiled his military bias,
For a good price, and then his work became
A reproduction of a reproduction
Issued in multiples, mail-ordered
All over childhood to the merry puzzlers.
You can open old wounds like a box,
That slow knitting of pictures and glory
In Tennessee and Massachusetts.
I hold an inch of space, the missing piece,
The notional and beautiful republic
Expressing what was fought for and who died,
'The last full measure of devotion . . .'
– Put hats on heads, place heads on fallen men
And resurrect the dead, the broken wheels:
A finished puzzle ends up in a dream,
A subterranean, consecrated picnic,
A hand waving in the fraternal paint.

Dieback

Eyes register their natural frontiers
Over invisible marathons, snakes, grasses,
Retreating to familiarity,
Imagination, mind, my feet and shoes.
This is oceanic country and I want a horse
And to be lonely, lawless and nomadic.
Beneath the Australasian blue
On the Tablelands, the dry pasturage
Rises and falls on continental cadences.
A lifetime dreaming of summers in Scotland
Brings me a big bag of blue childhood
But this is more of sky, an up-above
Illusory with yonder's blue beyond blue.
More birds enter my vocabulary
But I have no names by which to call them:
Eyes chronicle these things, all new to me,
Wordless in an optic archive.
I've seen the land and heard its native tongue,
But I'm its stranger, a pig-ignorant
Pedestrian, watching what he steps on.
Though I've been bumped into by a mad bat
With faulty radar, and bitten by a stoat
In Scotland, nature here is angrier
Than sanity can bear to contemplate.
I could do with grey-green gum-tree shade
And the perfumery of eucalypts,
But this is a landscape of dieback, trees
Whipped by bacterial artistry and flayed
Into nude postures, bark and leafage gone,
A famished gathering of naked Ys.

I can see five animals, including man
In a fast Japanese vehicle, spurting dust
With speed's up-tempo confidence.
Good State, what's stripped your forests bare,
What pastoral crime's been done to you
In this modernity, by carelessness
Or by sap-sipping, hungry beetles?
I haven't got the right, but I care.
Night falls here without sorrow. Truly, it falls
With howling innocence, cold and starry.
Under a slice of moon, the bald forests cry
Standing in their own coffins.

In the 1950s

The Courier was full of it. A whole page
Described the opening of the new transmitter,
Those who were there, how they were dressed, and who
Got up to speak and what they talked about.
He read it out to me, and I could tell
From his pauses, as I stood with my duster,
That soon we'd have one in our living room.
I could see myself cleaning it, wiping the screen,
Knowing the corner where I'd put the set
To best advantage, where he would sit, where I
Would sit, moving the chairs a few feet round
Away from the fire.
                              I missed the cinema.
Each Sunday I read out what was on that week,
And if he showed an interest, I'd learned
How he'd forget; or if one had a star
Or story that I knew he'd want to see,
He'd point out how it was too far away
With the last bus back at seven, his work
Such that he never had a Saturday
To himself, and the Roxy shut on Sundays.

I coaxed his willingness until I felt
A screenlight falling on our furniture;
And as he read out what the programmes were
I thought of how the wireless missed me out
As we sat, he listening or seeming to,
Me with my sewing as the fire collapsed
Down on its woody ash, and bedtime chimed
Its moment on the wedding-present clock.

[47]

Above the comedies, applause and news,
That world of people laughing in London,
I listened without listening and sewed.

It wasn't that we easily afforded one
Or that he had the sort of pride which made him
Pushy to buy the first set in our district.
Old Struthers ducked, trying to dodge the custard
Tossed by a funnyman in the slapstick.
'Nation', he quoted, 'shall speak peace unto nation.'
It was worth it, to see Anderson jealous –
His wife forbade it as the Devil's gadget –
With three tractors, a new car every year.
After that first few weeks of visitors
Eating my scones, my cherry cake and biscuits,
We sat in the dark, adjusting the light
By lamps and curtains . . . Contrast, Brightness,
The Vertical and Horizontal Holds:
He read the handbook like his *Scottish Farmer*.
I put my sewing down for a whole month.
We talked again, always of what we watched,
In that half hour of the cooling set.
His rural body leaned towards the screen
As if his promised 'window on the world'
Yielded too small a square of it, or gave
Too much of life beyond the one he lived.
And half the time his mouth hung open on
A wonder or resentment as he prowled
The screen, his eyes on all fours, watching, fooled
And frightened by those toffs 'in town tonight'.
Names that he couldn't talk to were his masters.
'Some day,' he said 'I'll take us both to London.'
Soon there were aerials on other roofs.
Each time I saw the van from the Clydesdale

I felt a little less alone
On summer evenings with the curtains drawn.
Then everybody had one. My husband watched
The War at Sea, and then *War in the Air*;
He brought two Irish workmen once, to watch
A match: they sat with their caps on their knees.

I watched the children's shows, and wept for me –
That puppet on the top of the piano!
After these years of news and Michelmore,
Of Gilbert Harding and the Weatherman,
I'd look south thinking that I knew the world
As I pegged my washing up against the wind.
And then the Sixties, the Seventies, changes
Our entertainment half-prepared us for,
New houses, each with its aerial
From the day it was built, supermarkets,
The Motorway and the Industrial Estate:
He looked at them and felt responsible.

Now, in The Home, I seek The Quiet Room,
Finding my friends there with their whist and wool.
It is so hard to be alone and quiet
These days, even here, where many are dying;
But sometimes, after reading, I go down
To watch the late-night widowers and widows,
Their papers folded at The Viewer's Page.
'We never see you in the TV Lounge.'
'No. No,' I say. 'I pick my programmes now.'

The War in the Congo

A man in a bar in Glasgow told me of how
He'd served with the Irish Army in the Congo
Under the flag of the United Nations.
'It was hot,' he told me, 'hot, and equatorial.'

They passed through a deserted and dog-ridden town.
They passed a house that had been blown up.
An arm, with a hand, rose between blasted breeze-blocks.
In the black hand was an envelope, between fingers and
                                                    thumb.

The Irish soldier looked at the hand and its letter.
Cement dust scabbed the blood on the arm.
He tore a corner off the envelope, removing the stamp,
Which he sent to his nephew in Howth, in Ireland.

In reply to what my companion asked him,
The soldier said it wasn't right to read a stranger's mail.
There was no one about in the little town, other than
Dogs and birds, and the arm and its hand, like a cleft stick.

He didn't say if it was the hand of a man or a woman
In which the letter was held, between fingers and thumb.
It was the arm of black Anon, of Africa,
Holding a letter, just received or unsent.

What concerns me is the soldier's nephew in Howth
Holding the piece of envelope with tweezers
Over the spout of a steaming kettle, and the stamp,
Renewed and drying between sheets of blotting-paper.

Philately of foreign wars is a boy in Howth
Licking a transparent hinge, and mounting a stamp
In his album, hot, hot and equatorial,
That innocent know-nothing stamp, lonesome in history.

Did he or she read it, that letter? Who wrote it? Who sent it?
So many stamps, and stamps from many countries,
And boys saying to their uncles and elder brothers,
'Remember, when you get there, to send me their stamps.'

4/4

in memoriam John Brogan

There was that night at pleasant Kate's
When you beat out your boogie'd bars
Among the bow-tied advocates
Swaying like minor characters
Of the Enlightenment, their laws
Dismantled by your drag and pause.
Your left hand's rhythmic boom and walk
Shivered the porcelain and crushed
Twelve strokes of midnight on the clock.
Even the chatterboxes hushed.
Like a young Hoagy Carmichael –
Thinking, smoking, drinking, sociable –
You used to stare out through your fug
With that half-smile of early wisdom,
Part intellectual, part rogue,
Pro life and *anti* tedium.
Here's to your memory, Jack,
Leaning into a whispered joke
Or a conspiracy against
Conservatives and sundry shits
Whose pranks or phoniness incensed
Distrust of the patriciates.
And here's to yesterday's State Bar
And to the socialism of pleasure;
Here's to that half-cut afternoon
Jamming at Jimmy's in Rutherglen
Until my beat-up tenor sax
Spat springs and pads, giving it max,
When Lithuania's silver flute
Whistled its lyric absolute.

Bohemians with haircuts, glass
In hand, the decent working-class
Created us for politics
In which we talked but couldn't lead,
Read poetry, played jazz instead,
Our undeclared republic's
Ferocity discussed and shelved
As notional and unresolved.
Strange how we served the cause of books:
Knowledge, a pike to stand behind
At barricades of love and mind –
Read this, and contradict the crooks!
This toast's to our librarianship –
I catalogue each taste and sip.
A drink, too, for our generation's
Withered ideals, that dwindled sense,
Sold out, tormented innocence
And salaried impatience.
So here's to booze's brotherhood
Puking on Ballageich Hill.
It didn't do us any good,
But what the hell, Jack, what the hell.

Maggie's Corner

Round and round, caught in a loop of film,
I walk ahead of who and where I am.
I turn the corner named for Maggie Earl.
The same old postbox reddens on her wall.

When Maggie ran Inchinnan's corner shop
Its stewed light was the shade of tinkers' tea.
Her corner keeps her name. It won't give up.
It smells of sweet-shop sugared memory.

Nostalgia's a bam. Distrust its stink.
Four decades old, and still that powerful dream
Pervades the mental twilight with its pink
Light-puddles on a rural housing-scheme.

I think of calls made from the corner's kiosk.
'Press *Button B*' and it's a wintry dusk.
A weathered, retrospective second-sight
Will see me catch the front-road bus tonight

With three half-crowns, a folded ten-bob note,
To buy the evening for a girl and me.
Here, everywhere, forethought and afterthought,
Nowhere and nothing's what I think I see,

Or what I thought I thought, or saw, no if
Or but about it, just the world I'm in.
My heart beats back and forth across a life
Bearing its spoon of blood like medicine.

Running the East Wind

It runs ahead of me on gaseous muscle.
It is the steep hill within me,
Planning my exhaustion.
Sleet and hail goad me like commissars.

It comes airmail from Murmansk
Leaving behind its scent of reindeer,
Its Lapp and Scandinavian accents,
Dropping its cold swords in the North Sea.

I do this for my health's sake
And because I used to like it, not for
Siberian sport, a spectral braggart
Showing off in its icy gymnasium.

A Syrian auxiliary felt this wind
On what was left of his sun-tan.
He listened to its half-Arctic jokes
Then slew the prisoners.

The Ice Queen is laughing at
My goose-bumps, my acidic saliva.
This wind is her regiment of snow-cossacks.
Wet life huddles in the hedgerows.

Coniferous Tentsmuir whistles in its forest.
I surrender, and the wind turns into swift urchins
Begging handouts from my breath.
They are stripping my lungs.

[55]

It turns again and pushes me like a pram.
It runs its fingers through my hair
Bearing me home on its transparent vehicles,
On its millions of glassy wheels.

In-flight Entertainment

Time lets its scientific minutes drop
On the Australian emptiness, a brown
Rugged geology where clocks are baked
In God's kiln, earthenware timepieces
Computing natural spans of insect life
Anticlockwise. Marginal nature gets by
Where there's no one to go for a walk with
And the first and last footprints slid under
Into deserted time and dry grottoes
Yesterday or millennia ago,
It makes no difference. That town beneath us,
Without buildings, fencing or municipality,
Might be the place called Nevermore, a dry
Republic ruled by solar plutocrats.
Some clown crossed it on camelback, others
Discovered the dotted line of their hot trek
Staggering over the unwritten map
Into a parched waterhole, imagining
Their own bones posed as they would leave them,
Deliberate, heroic litter,
Dissolving into horror, then into spirit.
So, better to sit up straight, back to a rock,
And hope for dignity in the annals,
A winged shadow casting its event of shade
To the cries of lost nomads and explorers.
    At thirty thousand feet, it's all go now
In our flying cinema. Earphones bring me
Time whiled away in in-flight entertainment.
I choose the channel called Heavenly Choirs
In the programme, but I'm in the wrong mood

For celestial flutes and the twanged God-harp
Concertos commissioned by the airline.
An Indonesian turbulence brings on
Spontaneous fidgeting with seat-belt buckles,
Ashtrays, and, in one case, a rosary.
It's as anxious as disaster's soundtrack.
My drink rumbas across its trembling tray.
Schooners on the Conradian sea and Dutch
East Indiamen race for the sheltered bays
Tiny under volcanoes, spice-bundles tied
In palm-roofed warehouses by windy wharfs.
Our big bird flutters its mineral feathers
Going down by invisible staircases
Through tropical rain, our slow descent driven
Straight to the shopkeepers of Singapore
And the days when I clerked for Stamford Raffles
In his turbanned garrison, mastering
Malay and opportunities of The Straits.
This airport doesn't feel like terra firma,
More like a space station, a half-way house
Between the stars and British history.

      Dark now, all the way to London, and sleep
Goes by me on its glass sails, not stopping
Throughout these pages of our *bon voyage*.
Over the Bay of Bengal, I walk down
Aromatic corridors, and India dozes
Beneath three hundred tons of rapid weight
And people crossing the world in three bounds.
I can see nothing but sacred darkness
On the underside of the wind, a glow
Where cloudy light describes a multitude
Dreaming in its city, its electric bowl.
I fall into a cultured quarter-sleep,
One eye half-open like a crocodile's.

[58]

Fictitious light squirms on the movie screen
But absentmindedness narrates another tale.
Reality's make-believe, and that's its point:
I've dreamt myself into mistaken times,
Not where I am, but all over the place.
The present's just as bad – the clock's going back,
But everyone's fixed to biological forwards.
Their destiny, like mine, is to grow old
As fate, or pilot error, has it, weather,
Metal fatigue, or ghostly horsemen from
The Mogul Empire, riding the stratosphere.
We're all travelling from the twenty-ninth
To the twenty-eighth, still living in
Yesterday, which takes us to Bahrain,
Where I have never been before. Pirates
On perilous star-dhows swing from the moon's
Islamic sickle, serious, cut-throat Sinbads.

     High over Babylon and Nineveh,
Ancient astronomers observe our lights;
Soothsayers with the troops of Alexander
Read our high thunder as a sacred omen.
I remember my classics teacher saying,
'Ah, yes, the Hittites . . . Who were the Hittites, boy?'
And there they are, the Hittites, one and all,
To say nothing of Midas, Mithridates,
Phrygia, Pontus and the satrapies
In Europe's Asian antithesis.
Where else should turn up next on my agenda
If not Byzantium outlined in neon
Advertisements, Marmora, Bosphorus?
Now that we're all awake, I hear a fool
Refer to down-below as Istanbul.
Where has he been for these past thousand years?

[59]

Miletus once was mighty, long ago.
I drag an adage over the Roman Empire,
Its winter vineyards, olive groves and highways,
Nocturnal autobahns, palatinates.
Night-lights in the European bedroom yield
To dawn and England in November.
Stiff knees and sleeplessness: I saw no God
In my internal flying-time throughout
These indoor hours at mighty altitude.
Those on the other wing can see the Thames,
Westminster foggy and Big Ben at seven.
Change terminals, change planes, process the bags,
This London never could be north enough
For me and who I love and travel with
And who has slept through half of geography.

The Departures of
Friends in Childhood

With optimism at the thrill of it –
The rarity of a taxi, suitcases stowed
On the floorboards and the furniture sold –
They drove through green shadows at the ends of lanes
To where-you-will in every New-Found-Land,
Ontario, North Island, New South Wales.
And always our mothers would say, 'Give them
Something of yours, the thing you love best' –
An envied marble, the left-handed boxing glove –
Knowing that their mothers would say the same –
A triangular stamp, a lightweight Egyptian piastre;
And anyone with cash or curiosity
Attended the auctions of gardening tools,
Bicycles, wireless sets and the forlorn shoes.
Boys would fight for the last time and shake hands,
Our clumsily affectionate farewells!
'Goodbye,' girls said to each other, 'Goodbye.'
At the exchange of gifts, at tea-parties
Invented out of rationed tea and sugar,
There seemed the promise of love to others
Waiting for them in the lands of the atlas.
In a place they wouldn't recognize, the wind
In the remaining tree cries in its wisdom,
Its leaves repeating the summer noise for For Ever
To names I can't remember as I listen to
Emigrant songs, the sundered families.
One butterfly where once there were so many.

The Dark Crossroads

Its small door asks its customers to stoop.
    Inside, a redesigned antiquity
Reproaches strangers entering to quench
    A travel-thirst or drouth of field-labour.
No rural innocents: ale-tinted light
    Died long ago behind the paneling
And that hand-painted sign above the door –
    The licensee's name drawn in Georgian cursive –
Fakes yesteryear as neatly as tankards
    Hooked in commemorative pewter rows.
Horse-brasses, warming-pans, foxed sporting prints,
    Yeomanry carbines crossed above the hearth,
Depict quondam society, preserved
    In the shadows of low-ceilinged aforetime,
Sweat's trinketry and souvenirs of servants,
    Billhooks of hedgers, rural militia's
Sabres, and a framed box of brass buttons.
    Men in blazers, hacking jackets, cravats,
Tweeds, suede shoes and cavalry twill trousers,
    Preside with gin, the diehards of opinions
Made in this place. A regimental tie
    Addresses me and tries to weigh my mind
Through sockets of its death's head insignias.
    The publican is Wing Commander X
Standing beside two sleeping Dobermanns.
    Five words have uttered who I am and where
I come from, like a paragraph: scoundrels,
    Tenements, drunkenness, their false Scotland.
You don't speak back in this company, unless
    You want to feel imaginary rope

[62]

Around your neck at the dream-gallows
    Carpentered quickly by a psychopath
Sanctioned by his satanic magistrates.
    I am an uppity Jock without valour,
Not lacking, though, in discretion, here,
    Where cavaliers bluster over thinned spirits
With fossilized, sinister gaiety.
    I find a snug corner. A pint of beer
Helps me to while away an English hour
    Until the bus that starts my journey home
Arrives nearby, at a stop where a man
    Sits on a stone with his newspaper, flask
And sandwiches, a woman with a caged hen
    Observing sixty minutes dwindle on
Her wristwatch, hidden by a tight, tugged sleeve.
    I picture what it looks like from outside –
The thatch, the whitewash and the mullioned windows
    Negotiating eighteenth-century trust,
A rendezvous with ordered permanence,
    As they might see it, crowded at the bar,
Turning to look at me. One man goes through
    His repertoire of 'Scotsmen I have known'.
I'm meant to hear. The calculated voice
    Distributes mirth, rakish jocosity
Bred in the hearty schools of prejudice.
    'Their place,' I warn myself. 'Leave it alone.'
But I do this, this notional revenge,
    A necessary act of wickedness
As pride humps ire, of which I am not proud.
    History moves against us once again.
Voice-niggers and any-shade victims of skin
    Devise their slave revolts, indigenous
Dreams of the moss trooper, the righteous horseman.
    Disturbed by bad aggrandizement, theirs, mine –

[63]

Unwanted thoughts, but unaccountable –
    I stand in fine rain watching dust curdle.
When privileged disdain mounts its high horse,
    Testing the stirrups, the sabre's edge,
It's time to mount your own, hearing the note
    That gathers schiltrons to the wapinschaw,
Though these are words and obsolete signals
    Describing a defensive hate, bloodlust
Soured into ink, a library carnage.

Memory and Imagination

Metre's continuum
Articulates
An artless view of water, sky and slates.
Rhythmical memory,
Archival drum,
Its hammer beats with primitive decorum
Over the roofs, past chimneypots
Toward the river's tidal pulse
Where wind-and-water's rituals
Invent and re-invent
Somnambulistic thoughts,
Chimeras, ecstasy, delirium,
The visionary and its sacrament.
Outlines of Buddon Ness,
The over-there,
Run through an optic repertoire,
Discoveries of eye and hand
Obedient to what's known or can be found,
Made visible and new and out of time
By ingenuity and stunts of rhyme,
Paint, pencil, three struck chords
Or washed-up stick
Scratched on the sand's
Moist, aromatic
Obliging grains,
Pictured geography
Etched in the fragrance of infinite sea.

Each thought and picture that our arts contrive
        Contributes to the day,
           A narrative
        Depicting chapters in
           A book of mind
        Read in at leisure by
           A browsing wind.
Passive adventure when the mind's let loose
Reanimates itself as active art:
     Though memory's an introvert
     Imagination shares its house
        In reason's spiritland
           Where lines are drawn
        By an ancestral hand.
Works that were made two thousand years ago
           Portray their age
        But do not cease to grow
In modified enchantment, like a tree's
Lifetime of lifetimes of its species.
        Seeing is disbelief
           And take here as
My instance: significant etceteras
           Assemble in
        Their ordinary shapes
           But mind can change
        Uncertain waterscapes.
        That coloured pool could be
           The Serchio's
        Displaced to Tay by quick
           Sight-echoes.
Hudson, Tiber, Seine and the Missouri
Exist in somewhere else's history,
        While metaphoric winds'
           Dramatic light

Translates imagination's second-sight
    Into a figured absolute
   Somewhere beyond perception or
        The brute
  Sensoria – for there, incensed,
        Occult,
Poseidon rises from where fresh meets salt
Into the arms of Tutha, Tay's goddess,
   North-water's Pictish Artemis
    Among her swimming stags,
      Otters,
     Seals and swans,
Columban saints who navigate on stones.
    Osiris with his black
     Nilotic fleet
    And Attic biremes on
     The water-street
  Glide by on muscled slavery,
      Whipped oars
    That drive Rome's polyglot
     Conquistadors.
And what I say I see is what is there,
   Liquid infinity's
    Far anywhere.

    Seen *contre-jour*
  At morning's Provençal
Disturbed location, supernatural
   Memory takes me there,
    I don't know why:
Ligurian turquoise in a Scottish sky,
A whitewashed lighthouse and an early yacht
Mysteriously Aegean and remote.
    Who cares what year it is

[67]

When what you see
Turns parish, river and chronology
Into the inside-out of Caledonia's
Cognitive acres stripped of time and laws?
Not caring where or when you are
Upsets
Responsibility,
But mind forgets
Its sordid selfishness
And these are sane
Routines,
Remembering delight and pain,
If only sometimes for an hour or two
When there is nothing else to do.
Logic and purpose slip
Into non-literal scholarship
Where memory invents to repossess
Utopian, meditative peace,
Increase
In an aesthetic universe
Pulled in a smooth, iambic hearse
Until the weight of centuries
Makes sense,
Informs the present, then
The future tense.
Past, guide
My eye, my hand,
And make me new;
Open your mausoleums and subdue
Novelty's blandishments. Eternal stories
Describe their news and mysteries;
Transfigured fact and elevated dream
Perpetuate their metrical verbatim
Into the metronomic clock

Where here
Meets there
And now meets then,
That hard frontier
Where pencil, paint, wood, stone
And numbered rhyme
Converse with music on the edge of time.

A still boat preens
Its sunken duplicate
In an aquatic foreground's self-portrait
Erased by ripples, reinstated by
A radiant renewal in the sky.
An unimagined, unremembered boat,
Undreamt, reality
As anecdote,
Obsesses me, until
The mirror's mirrored,
Reflection's replicas,
Remembrance, stirred
By memory,
Imagination, dream,
And self's transformed
Into its anonym.
Within that psyche, sight, touch, smell and sound
Create the taste
Of something that's beyond
Quick understanding: dusk
Rubs light against
A cloudy pink,
And sky's experienced
Formations re-enact
A Pictish beauty
As the reflected West bleeds on the Tay;

[69]

A cool wind from the East
Disturbs a tree
And strokes the cheek
With memory
While summer's roses stir
Religious scents
Into invisible
Sniffed sacraments;
And, from an open window, Mozart's strings
Encourage echoed songs,
Thrush-throats,
Thrush-wings.
Alluded nature, quoting from a quote,
Returns the symphony
To its wood-note,
Line to the eye
And back again,
The wind
Into a reminiscence of a hand:
Gives back to gardens the Edenic rose
Quotidian to the gardener's nose;
Eye, nose, skin, ear,
Reverberate on the vernacular,
And they become a taste,
A savoury
Embodiment,
A sense, a memory
In all dimensions of the sentient,
Sight, sound, touch, taste and smell,
Imagination's immortelle.

An Address to Adolphe Sax in Heaven

For Ted Tarling

That your great gift to human ears
Offended purist connoisseurs
Might not be weird, but that's the word
They thought described the sound they heard.
Though Berlioz defended it
Most maestros reprehended it,
While Richard Wagner's saxophobics
Call for a mouthful of aerobics –
Rassenkreuzungsklangwerkzeuge.
Unrhymable! It's on its own,
Your 'instrument of hybrid tone'.
Bizet in his *L'Arlésienne* –
A sound like lyric Caliban –
Raised eyebrows as he lowered the tone
With solos for a saxophone.
Parisian social experts feared
The sound of sex was what they heard,
Melodic monsters, Minotaurs,
Breaking down their bedroom doors.
Its complicated *quidditas*
Prognosticated future jazz.
Not what you had in mind, *cher Sax*:
Concertos, not yackety-yaks,
Were more your forte. You would love
The alto one by Glazunov,
Ibert's, or Pierre Max Dubois's
Alto-harmonious noise.

Bordellos and the regiments
Took greatly to your instruments.

[71]

Your lacquered cosmopolitans
Marched under hot, colonial suns,
And, in a room behind the bar
In Senegal or Côte d'Ivoire,
Melodies no conservatoire
Would ever countenance were played –
A Guadeloupan serenade
Or tune to set the heart astir
In an outpost of Madagascar.
Saharan saxophones! Annam
Transfigured by their 'priestly calm'!

Think of the clarinets of France
With instrumental reverence! –
Hyacinthe Klosé and Leblanc,
Their breath, the fingerprints of song!
What better mouth as embouchure
Than one that says the word *amour*
Or when the clarinet's played low
Describes its sound as *chalumeau*?
Its 'simple system,' you, Sax, built –
So-called because it's difficult –
Found favour, but the laws of patent
Failed to discourage disputant
Competitors and plagiarists,
Invention's parasitic pests.
Not, though, your seven-belled trombone
That looked like the first telephone
Exchange, your *saxotromba's* freak
Ingenious *saxomblatarique*.
That elephantine hearing-aid
Ruptured and deafened those who played,
Or tried to, its enormous tones'
Almighty bass convulsions.

Critical slander and derision
Postponed, but couldn't halt, your mission.
Low audiences applauded it
And your alumni in the pit
Stood up and wiped wine-sweaty brows
Taking their own, and their master's, bows.
You hoped for an orchestral glory;
Destiny wrote another story –
Hack-blowers in the Music Hall
And quick-march guardsmen in the Mall:
Ignored for a symphonic part
You put an *oompah* into art.
Ballroom, night-club and bawdy-house
Were futures for your posthumous
Discovery, the sound of feet
Dancing and tapping, indiscreet
Lyricism in the glowing smoke,
Venereal riffs and blue heartache
In Harlem or in *Barrowland*
Where half the orchestra were canned.
So, Sax, profanity's the fate
Your instruments negotiate
Through New Orleans to Buddy Tate
While saxophonic venery's
Libidinous communiqués
Disclose that St Cecilia's just
A woman when it comes to lust.
From Buffs and Garde Républicaine
To Charlie Parker and Coltrane!
Trambauer, Hawkins, Chu and Bechet,
Lester, Sims and Cohn, and Wardell Gray,
Hodges, Webster, Rollins, Getz,
Lucky, Lockjaw, Dexter, Konitz
Brought oompah'd art to that fine pitch

Where music's an erotic itch
A fingernail's too blunt to scratch.
But Arnold Bennett thought his ear
Affronted by the tunes of beer.

Now look at you! From Aberdeen
To hamlets in the Argentine,
In Reykjavik and Birmingham,
Djakarta and Dar es Salaam,
High-stepping bands with majorettes
Play saxophones like martinets.
Your beggar with its inbuilt bowl's
Played in the cause of rock 'n' roll's
Electric millionaires, subfusc
Wee buggers with an urge to busk.

A genius who invents a noise
Adds to the store of sonic toys
That *Homo ludens* in his wisdom
Accepts into his playful system.
Adolphe, once close to suicide,
Cher maître, take your place beside
Celebrity whose household name
Is dictionaried in its fame –
Derrick, the hangman, Heinz's beans,
Kellogg's cornflakes, Levi's jeans,
Ford of the cars and Louis Braille,
Freud, Epicurus, Chippendale,
Marx and the verse Petrarch devised,
Martini, and the pasteurized,
Newtonian Law, the arch of Goth,
Mackintosh's sea-proofed cloth,
And Wellington, he of the boot,
Good, optimistic King Canute,

Fabian's tactics, Mills' bomb,
The Midas touch, Brummell's aplomb,
Platonic love, Macadam's roads,
Several diseases, Pindar's odes,
Darwinianism, Cardigan,
And J. M. Barrie's Peter Pan.
From saxophone quartets by Strauss
On days off from the Opera House,
Or works by Milhaud and Ravel
Or Villa-Lobos in Brazil,
To Lester leaping in possessed
By his brass-belled iconoclast,
The sound we hear is yours, Adolphe,
Posterity, its howling wolf,
Time salivating on a reed
And fingering at breakneck speed.

The Country Kitchen

Madame Moulinier used to bring
Two rabbits a week, and two hens,
Still warm, but throttled. The kitchen's
Cutlery lacked a decent knife
But I did the best I could, wishing
There was an animal-opener
The equal in convenience
To what you'd use on a tin of beans.
Blood seeped from the blunt incisions.
Peeling each portion of their skins
The sounds were slight, but bad, and such
I had to shut my eyes and whistle.
It felt like pulling plasters off your leg –
The pain and noise of skin and hair.
The heads were worst of all –
The ears, the eyes, the little mouths.
Blood leaked from the drainpipe.
The house was bleeding.
As for the hens, I plucked feathers
Among the trees, beyond the house.
It took most of an afternoon.
It looked like an Indian massacre
When I'd finished – shattered head-dresses.
We cooked them in the big pot, *sauvage* –
Shallots, a muslin bag of herbs
Gathered from the neglected gardens.
Some of these herbs were weeds and grasses.
The dug garlic was green, but good.
So was the garnish of young chives.
On evening walks, I used to watch

The rabbits stare back from their hutch,
Wondering which bunny was next;
And the hens pecking white dirt – *dot, dot,*
And then the scare of a footstep.
I asked a peasant to sharpen my knife
On the stone he used for his scythe.
It made it easier, and it didn't –
My hand inside a hen's dead warmth,
Or slitting open the rabbits,
My wife saying, 'Keep the kidneys!' –
Amateur kitchen pathology.
So I said, 'I'm sick of rabbit;'
And, 'Another hen and I'll cluck!'
That village is announced by a fine sculpture.
A stone woman holds a stone child.
The woman's name is 'Abondance'.
I saw abundance all right:
In her stone bowls were stone vegetables,
Chiselled salads, a petrified artichoke.
I looked with envy at the walnut trees
Flourishing in botanical liberty.
The fishmonger's van was maritime,
Cold, dripping with melting ice,
An edible museum of the sea.
For nights on end I dreamt of close quarters
Boxed behind the nailed mesh,
Creeping backwards into furred heat,
Packed eyes and lettuce breath,
When ringed fingers dropped in
On a carnivorous visit.

Tremors

One stopped his hoe. Another slowed his rake.
I shuddered with the shudder, foot on the fork,
The tines of which chimed in the earth: earthquake
Or sonic boom or nuclear mistake.
Four Tayport gardeners looked up from their work.
It scattered birds and cats ran mad, then hid
In the shrubbery as a slate slid
From next door's roof and aerials were seen
To quiver, while a fourth man froze in mid-
Push of his wheelbarrow, its squeak a mean
Remark on tremors running up our legs.
Earth shifted by an inch. Tilth on a row
Landslided on the seeds. An earthen echo
Followed a chaffinch to its trembled eggs.

The Patrol

Last year, behind my house, against a wall,
I found four soldiers lounging on the grass
I hadn't cut. From fifty films I knew
That they were out of date. Their corporal
Sat in a weary sleep, helmet askew
And daisies in his hand, downheartedness
In how he rested underneath the tree.
Better not stay, I thought, but I couldn't
Prevent myself. They looked like history
Improved beyond cenotaphs, each man a saint
In a dented tin hat, his uniform
That had been in the clock and known the worm.
Why come back? Why rest here? Why anywhere?
A rifle's imprint stops grass growing there.

Adventure's Oafs

Our Territorials rehearse their street-
By-street and house-by-house control of towns.
The enemy's within; it's us, mincemeat
Already, butchered, us, the sly unknowns,
A two-up cock-y'r-snook electorate
Disgruntled that the mighty X installed
The government a quarter voted for.
If he'd do that – that boot-dismantled door –
He'd do it to his daddy's. Obdurate
Scots, stubborn apathy turns wet and cold
As weather, and you can get used to its
Self-loathing climate – see no Englishman,
Hear no monarchy's monkey make you run
To fetch and carry his prerequisites.
Your neighbour riding in The False Dragoons
Praises a nephew on the Ness with guns
Where officers with wee field telephones
Direct their men against ludic revolt's
Imaginary pikes and catapults.
Proverbial gangling youth drops hand grenades
Through glassless windows. Adventure's oafs,
Good soldiers, patriots or renegades –
Whatever motive, theirs or mine – enough's
Enough of make-believe when who you'd shoot
Might be the man next door. What's absolute
In nations? No one knows, though any fool
Can feel their differences when treason's pull
Sets up its heave between the status quo
And who you'd rather be and when. Occult
History makes the answers difficult:

It's yesterday; tomorrow's not tomorrow.
So carry your kicked arse in a wheelbarrow.
You're colonized! Maybe you didn't know?
Who are the traitors, us, or Unionists
In uniform, the foederati? Fists
Toil in the dream, furniture barricades
Go up on paper while homespun brigades
Muster in corners where the bad meets worse.
Civil Insurgency! The Trojan Horse!
It's hand-to-hand inside the dummy house.
Upstairs, they find their scarecrow Minotaurs,
Rebels of straw, innocent, infamous.